Sitting on the Farm

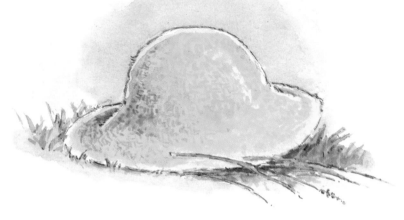

by Bob King

illustrated by Bill Slavin

ORCHARD BOOKS

New York

Text copyright © 1991 by Oak Street Music
Illustrations copyright © 1991 by Bill Slavin
First published in Canada by Kids Can Press Ltd.
Kids Can Press Ltd. acknowledges with appreciation the assistance of the Canada Council
and the Ontario Arts Council in the production of this book.
First American edition 1992 published by Orchard Books

Orchard Books
387 Park Avenue South
New York, NY 10016

Manufactured in the United States of America
Printed by General Offset Company, Inc.
Bound by Horowitz/Rae
Book design by Susan Phillips
The text of this book is set in 23 point ITC American Typewriter Medium Condensed.

10   9   8   7   6   5   4   3   2   1

Library of Congress Cataloging-in-Publication Data
King, Bob.
    Sitting on the farm / written by Bob King ; illustrated by Bill Slavin. — 1st ed.
        p.   cm.
    Summary: A girl trying to get a little bug off her knee enlists the aid of a series of
increasingly larger animals.
    ISBN 0-531-05985-5. — ISBN 0-531-08585-6 (lib. bdg.)
    [1. Animals—Songs and music.   2. Songs.]   I. Slavin, Bill, ill.   II. Title.
PZ8.3.K567Si   1992
782.42164'0268—dc20   91-17253

To my son, Kris

—B.K.

For my parents, Bill and Dorothy

—B.S.

Sitting on the farm, happy as can be,

I had a little bug on my knee.

I said, "Hey, Bug, get off my knee."

Well, that old bug said, "No siree!"

So I picked up the telephone.

I called my friend the frog at home.

I asked if she would like some lunch.

The frog came over and...

MUNCH!
MUNCH!
MUNCH!

Sitting on the farm, happy as can be,

Now I had a frog on my knee.

I said, "Hey, Frog, get off my knee."

Well, that old frog said, "No siree!"

So I picked up the telephone.

I called my friend the snake at home.

I asked if he would like some lunch.

The snake came over and...

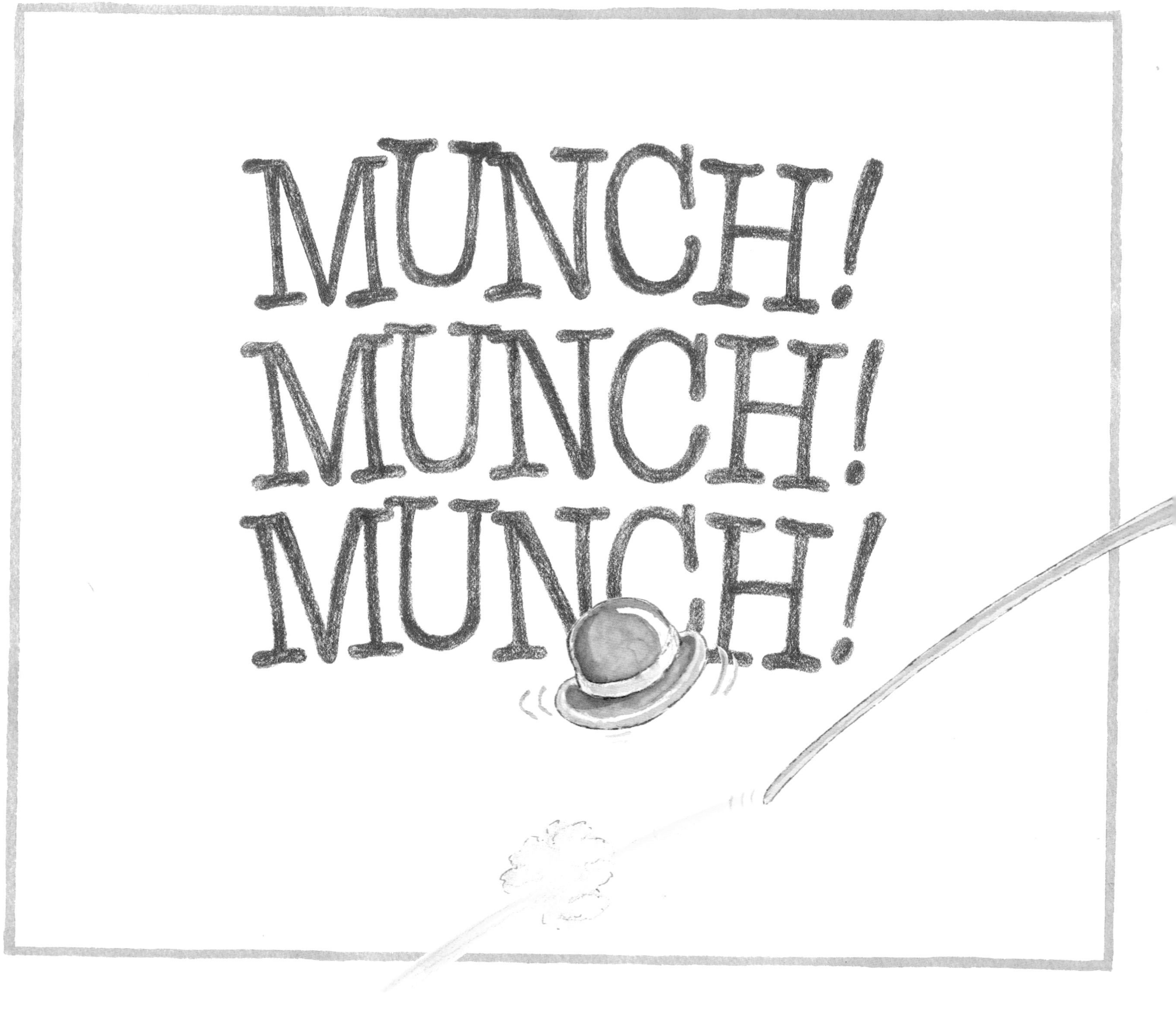
MUNCH!
MUNCH!
MUNCH!

Sitting on the farm, happy as can be,

Now I had a snake on my knee.

I said, "Hey, Snake, get off my knee."

Well, that old snake said, "No siree!"

So I picked up the telephone.

I called my friend the rat at home.

I asked if he would like some lunch.

The rat came over and...

MUNCH!
MUNCH!
MUNCH!

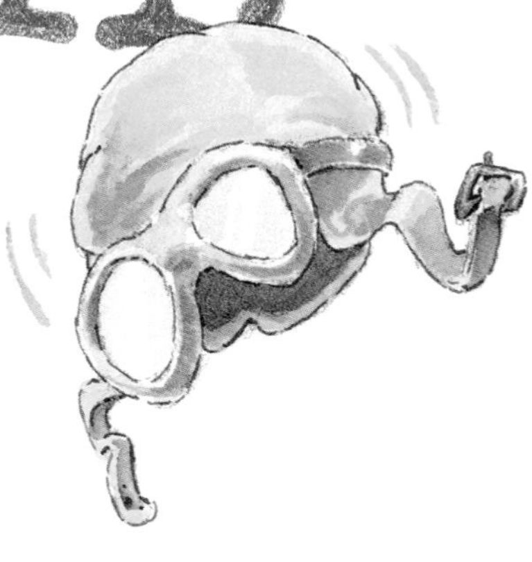

Sitting on the farm, happy as can be,

Now I had a rat on my knee.

I said, "Hey, Rat, get off my knee."

Well, that old rat said, "No siree!"

So I picked up the telephone.

I called my friend the cat at home.

I asked if she would like some lunch.

The cat came over and...

MUNCH! MUNCH! MUNCH!

Sitting on the farm, happy as can be,

Now I had a cat on my knee.

I said, "Hey, Cat, get off my knee."

Well, that old cat just looked at me.

So I picked up the telephone.

I called my friend the dog at home.

I asked if he would like some lunch.

The dog came over and...

MUNCH! MUNCH! MUNCH!

Sitting on the farm, happy as can be,

Now I had a dog on my knee.

I said, "Hey, Dog, get off my knee."

Well, that old dog said, "No siree!"

So I picked up the telephone.

I called my friend the bear at home.

I asked if she would like some lunch.

The bear came over and...

Sitting on the farm, happy as can be,
Now I had a bear on my knee.
I said, "Hey, Bear, get off my knee."
Well, that old bear said, "No siree!"
So I picked up the —

Won't somebody please help me
Get this bear off my knee....

Sitting on the Farm

Sitting on the farm, happy as can be, I had a little bug

on my knee. I said, "Hey, Bug, get off my knee." Well, that old bug said,

"No siree!" So I picked up the telephone, I called my friend the

frog at home. I asked if she would like some lunch, The frog came over and . . .

MUNCH! MUNCH! MUNCH!